When The Sun
Touched The River

JEFF EDRICH

Also by Jeff Edrich

———————————————

Dream of Broken Feathers
Iron in the Country

Available from Amazon.com books
Visit website: www.jeffedrich.com
Email: jeff.edrich@yahoo.com

For The Angel
That Came

***

When the bonds we knitted
have become a memory

we shall know
what utter grace it was
to have loved one another

***

Acknowledgements:

Thanks to Steve Haggerty,
Linda Shaw,
Heather Fullerton,
Jennifer Ciotta,
Vincent T. Dacquino,
the Mahopac Writers Group,
and all my friends who have given me
so much comfort and support.

CONTENTS

I

Everything I will give you…
The water, the sun
and one another.

I Am Making This Fire for You

I am making this fire for you.
If you could look through the many trees,
you would see my hands gathering stones
from the river and branches from the ground.

If you could look through the hills and mountains,
you would see my bones kneeling to the sun god,
finding the lost arrows, planting seeds in the valley.

If you could listen across the fields,
you would hear my voice singing...
My little leaf, my tree, my wings above the earth.

The wind blows this day home,
and the still mountain sleeps.
The long black night leaves its stars
in the shallows of the river.

Breath moves my hands.
I peel the thin branch, stripping its bark.
It is soft and smooth underneath.

I am close to the ground,
drawing a line between here and the clouds,
setting a mark to point to the fertile places.

Ancestors pull at my skin and wash my hair gray.
"Come," they say.

"I am not ready!" I laugh and dance until
they smile and give me twenty moons more.

I dance and they tell me
where the second current of the river lies,
and where the hidden breeze of your soul has blown,

and I find it,
on the top of a boulder where it is scooped out like a bowl,
filled with water from the rain.

In the still water I can see your face, looking to the sun.

"Looks To Sun," is your name.
I drink the water and know what to do.

I talk to the sun for days and nights,
even when it is hiding, I am talking.
And finally the sun says,

"I cannot rest with you talking to me all the time,
even when I get into my bed below the mountain
and cover my hot bones with night's cool stillness,
you are keeping me awake!"

And the sun gives me a part of its burning light,
and that is when it happens.

Our children ask if you found me in the sky or the river.

I laugh when you tell the story
of how I found you in the water in the bowl of the boulder,
of how it told me the secret of your name,
and how the wind of your spirit jumped into my heart.

I Love You

I have taken my clothes off.
I have placed my heart on the table.
I have placed my bones in the earth.
I have opened my spirit into the wind.

I have only one thing left.
The memory of you.

Without my clothes,
without my heart,
without my bones,
without my spirit,

I have only one thing left.
I love you.

Your Heart in the Wind

Walking through my blood,
your footsteps pound my heart.
I breathe your breath in the night of my sleep.

And then... morning comes,
painting her sacred light,
warming the grass and my skin,

and... I see...
there, across the river...
smoke...rising... in the distance.

I open my wings to come to you,
but stumble and fall,
forgetting, I am still a man.

By the edge of the water, I build a fire.
My heart is in the smoke.
Did you see it?
Is your head turned away from the river?

I am building the raft,
tying the strong branches together,
sighting a path across the water.

When the moon is bright like day I will cross.
With corn and turnips in the basket,
and skin from the deer of the forest,
I will come...

Whispering...
like the wind through the tall grass...
whispering...your name.

Across the River

The bear yawns from the long winter,
the fish move silently under the sun of spring.
I wake in the forest.

When it is quiet I ask the sun, "Where is she?"
"No one can find her," the sun says.

I am breathing the blood and bones of her life,
hearing the sound of her voice.

We are the birds migrating home,
the rains covering the heartland,
the wildflowers and pounding hooves.

I descend into the valley
and stand by the edge of the river.
"Where is she?" I ask.
The river answers, "You must find her."

I wait under the sun.
I wait for the wind to bring her scent.
I ask, without the sound of words, I ask.

Shadows of branches rest on my arm.
The mountain is still.
A leaf falls from the old tree across the river.

I call to the tree,
"Why have you let go of your child?"
The old tree does not answer.
The young leaf falls to the ground.

There,
across the river,
where the leaf has fallen,
She is searching for me.

In the deep of the forest,
the animals raise their heads from the ground and listen.
She is breathing the blood and bones of my life.

We spill across the valley.
The river pounds against its banks.

We are the birds migrating home,
the rains covering the heartland,
the wildflowers and pounding hooves.

Trust Your Heart

Trust your heart,
I will be soft,
I will be gentle.

I will see with clear eyes
what vulnerable beauty,
like all of Nature's giving hope,
rests, sacred.

Lay down naked,
unclothed,
untied from fear,
untied from time.

Reach out with the soft heat of your life
and I will wash you with my gentle hands.

You, who bring life to earth,
you who give birth to our days,

your soft shape,
like the soft shape of earth.

I will untie myself from fear and time
and breathe your scent
and kiss the flowers opening inside your heart.

Your Picture

You are gathering the deepest threads,
weaving them into soft blankets,
reaching into the earth,
drawing life into the world.

Your head is tilted with gentle acceptance
and your eyes open like the welcoming sea.

Are you a mother, or a girl wishing upon the stars?
Are you the lioness of the jungle,
or the wise woman of the tribe?
Are you the slave owned by unjust masters,
or a queen, returning to the world?

And how did the sun and the moon
draw the weaving hands of your heart
towards the open soul of mine?

Was it the fire you labored in like the goddess slave,
or the desert of loneliness wide as the earth?
Who saw the signs of your hands,
and the aching cross of my heart?

I cannot answer and thank the gods and the tides,
for the current of will that flowed across our path,
and for the wings that carried us home.

You may be an artist and a mother and a dreamer,
but most of all you are alive,
and holding your gifts in my hand
is like a golden day that I will breathe in forever.

I Listen

I listen to the shape of you,
to the shadows resting on your arm,
to the position of your head when you speak,
of running through the barren plains.

Your spirit comes while we are sitting in the field
and silently utters the ancient prayer.

Who will open
the heart of the cold ground?
Where is the soft field of sun
and the sparkling stream?

My mother, my father,
I cannot hold my wings open any longer.

Oh, how you walked over the sharp rocks and wept,
how you crossed the water and sky,
and flew high above the fires,
searching for home.

Your stories glow,
like lightning wrapped around your skin.
I am captive to the pictures in your eyes.

I listen to the shape of you,
reading the wind
in the curve of your shoulder,
touching the mountain
in the bones of your face.

I listen to the arch of your back,
to the fingers splayed open when you tell
of how your strength faded
and the rivers carried you home.

And now I know
why your hair falls like water,
and why the flesh adorns your bones
like the light of silver mornings,

and why the trees are strong
beneath their gentle leaves,
and why your words and stories
flood the space between our hands.

You are the silence of the falling snow,
the roar of the lioness.
I listen to the shape of you.

On the Wings of Morning

I dream of the sun coming over the mountain,
of touching your hand.

It is so beautiful to wake
and find you breathing by my side.

Your warm skin, your breath,
so much of you rising and falling
like pure innocence
sparkling on the current
of the river.

Even the sun holds its breath
and gently brushes your face,
trying not to wake you.

In this sacred moment,
the river lifts out of its banks
and runs under my skin
and you begin to smile
before your eyes are open.

Shard of Sun

The raw hunger of your love
tore itself out from its prison,
naked and pure,
wild and unleashed,
like a tidal wave in a hurricane,

your love
splayed me to the wall,
as you threw yourself against my life
crushing every bone.

Throw me upon the earth,
pour sparks into my veins,
run my blood like the rapids
and press the heat of your sun
until we are ashes.

Bounding Over the Fields

The wind and water call,
asking us to return what was given.
As if we had taken the sun
and sailed higher than the clouds.

"The rivers of your blood are our rivers!" they shout.
"The breath of your life is our breath!"

We laugh, "Our blood and breath are ours for this life,
ours for as long as we can make heat with our flesh!"
And we pour our hot blood into one another
and erupt into flames.

The wind and water call out again,
"That is our fire! Our blood!"

We laugh,
"Take it back if you can!"
and rush from the cliffs as roaring waterfalls,
and paint our orange glow across the sky.

The Heat of Her

How thankful I am for the heat of her.
For her soft giving thighs wrapped around mine
like the warm mountain in spring
pushing down on the soft meadow.

Like rivers pulled into the ocean,
our blood knows where to go
and flows into our union.

It sings the ancient chant
from within her to within me
and we hold one another like tree and earth.

It pounds inside our skin like a tribal drum,
dancing around the fire
and thunders until the sky cracks open.

Gasping for breath,
captive in one another's arms,
panting like animals running,
alive with the fire of earth.

Layers

There are so many layers of us spread across
the grass and in the sky and in the cities.
They're in the pages of books
and on the screens of movie theaters.

And in our dreams
walking hand-in-hand.

So many layers of the soft day rising.

Like little puppy dogs lifting their heads
from sleep close to their mother.
Like flowers lifting their heads
from sleep in the giving earth.

And like you lifting your head
feeling the soft layers of sun
bathing your skin.

Under the Tree

I love her hips, her shape,
softly holding the space within.

She walks with the grace of her melancholy.
She walks with her aches and laughter.

We live by the shining lake
and pull each other
across the grass to the old tree.
She leans back.

I am like a young boy
leaning against her soft body,
holding her face,
drinking her.

She laughs and mumbles,
"Mmmm..." through my mouth on hers,

and I cannot remember anything
except her shining through my skin.

Raspberries

They are in a round bowl on my kitchen counter.
Who put them there?
Glistening softly, beckoning and delicate,
like little hearts waiting.

I remember raspberries I picked once.
How warm and sweet that day was.

My dog was alive then.
We'd walk out to the backyard,
and eat the raspberries together.

And here they are, on the kitchen counter.
Did my love put them there for me?

But we have only talked.
We talked about raspberries,
about how we love them.

I think I love her,
but I told her I love raspberries,
she said she loves them too.
I wonder if she loves me.

I told her if she ever needed anything,
the key was under the couch in the hall.

I wonder how far she had to come,
to find my home, and my little room,
and the key under the old sofa in the hall.

And what she must have thought
when she saw my life waiting for her.

For You   *Written by the Angel*

I walked into your room
surveyed the simplicity,
a neatly made bed,
the lack of clutter--
A room like a monk's studio,
an austere cocoon.

I left the berries on the counter,
a bright spot of color
an explosion of flavor
and opened your mind
to receive the sensuous pleasures
of the physical world.

Soon, flowers appeared daily,
colorful artwork covered your mantle,
love notes sprinkled the surfaces,
and your closet brimmed with
fancy clothing.

You'd walk into the
heat of your room and it would
feel like the tropics,
the ceiling fan wafting breezes.

Instead of a drab monk's life
you opened your arms
to a colorful, rich, warm
love that swirled around you
like ocean waves.

You and I swam together
and drank the elixir of love
and ate fruit and cheese
and shared ourselves.

Anchor

When the earth first turned and anchored its place,
the sun finally had enough time to warm it up.
And every turn brought a new day.

When I saw you, I dropped an anchor,
and you did too, so that we wouldn't drift away.

And everywhere we went
was like walking into the first day of our life,

and we'd drop an anchor
so we could always pull ourselves back
to those beautiful memories.

And there were so many,
like the library where we met,
the space where we made love,
the path we used to walk,
and even the song we heard one day.

We found a way to anchor ourselves
to the bright spark within that song
and we could hold the rope and pull ourselves back
singing every word.

And we pulled ourselves back to
the day in the marketplace where we held hands
and bought gifts for each other.

And once,
we stood in the center of the wide field holding one another,
and the sun and the sky wrapped their arms around us.

We dropped our last anchor there and floated away.

We no longer needed to be anchored
by the memory of things we did
or hold onto ropes to pull ourselves back.

We were anchored to one other
by the love in our hearts
and nothing could pull us apart.

Swimming

The sun is so excited this morning.
Oh, how fine this day is
as breath wakes us into life,

and dreams circle,
like little fish swimming,
and we hook hope and reel in joy.

Oh, to feel so alive,
to have hands and feet,
to stand on the shore and cast out our reel
and perhaps even find love swimming in the water.

Angel

The angel carried the wounded bird,
the fish, and the flower.

We woke from darkness and knew,
she had brought us from the farthest reaches
where only weeping could be heard,

to a place called "The Light of Day,"
where it is always safe to open.

We will never forget the dark tunnel
and how far she had to go

and how she bent over us
and held our little heads

and how softly she put her hands
underneath our last breath

and how gently she flew
so she would not shake that last breath out of us

and placed us on the hillside
in the sun of day, in the lake, wind and earth

and we could smell the sweetness
and let go of the old sorrow we had held for so long.

You call with silent waves
until my last latch opens,

and the old sun of the forest,
lifts over the mountain
and spills out like honey.

I was full

but now I am brimming over.
I understood life,
but now it is radiant with meaning.

I was walking the path,
but now it is glowing.
I was content,
but now I am shining like the sun.

The Power of Your Name

Like starving and finding food,
or burning and jumping into the water,
the power of your name
resonates like a lifetime of heartbeats
rushing through my own.

I am awakened,
brought to tears,
and made to laugh.

They are the most beautiful letters
when they appear.
I am dissolved,
like standing before God
in a rush of light and joy.

Offering

Where does it come from?

Is it inside the little space in the flower?
Or is it between the tree and the lake?
Does it come only when we are sleeping?
Or is it in the heat under your skin?

I am not sure of many things,
but in the scattered attempts to live and breathe,
I will tell you what happened.

I held your hand,
and knew eternity was smiling.

I could feel your heat,
and I knew I would live forever.

And I didn't need to wonder
about the universe anymore,
or what stars were,
or what happens after we die,
because,

I found where it comes from.
I would look in your eyes,
and every question was answered.

Morning

I get up for a moment, and then snuggle back
in between the wall and her body, holding her
from behind, feeling warm like a toaster with the
orange glow of the universe burning.

And there in the warm heat, the gentle
acquiescence of her soft flesh, I rest beside her,
holding her bosom and the round curve of her
thigh, her womanly warm shape, her beauty, until
she stirs and grumble mumbles through a
cobwebby scratchy throat, "Good morning,
Sweetie," and I can hear the pure heart like a
golden sparrow singing through and know that is
the reason I am beside her.

The golden sparrow of her voice, her heart, her
soul, singing a dusty croaky, "Good morning,
Sweetie," clothed in the history of every step ever
climbed until now she rests here like a bar of gold
made flesh and a dream turned into a head with
golden hair and blue eyes and slightly parted lips
like the surrender of light.

And so I ask her something and she responds like
a flower blooming in my arms and the sun agrees
and sparks its long straight rays into the room,
touching the orchids and leaves and lighting her
beautiful hair and I press my face into her and
know I am holding the goddess and must now and
forever draw and write and sing of this moment
radiating into each other, burning like two candles
in the center of the world.

$\mathcal{Y}$our warmth

is like my oldest dream coming to find me
and my newest dream taking me home

like every part falling away from its bone
like the warm wet sweat of desire opening its wings

like gentle hands that will not let me go
pulling me back over and over.

$\mathcal{T}$he birds have come to the edge of the window.

The foxes have come out of their dens.
The grass is waving under the wind.

"Wake, my darling," the sun whispers.

The leaves of the willow brush your face,
and the river washes your skin,

and in the light of morning even the yellow petals
are singing your name.

Before We Touch

There is no explanation for what happens
when you are near.

There is only you, standing there

and I, dissolving into a second body

passing through my skin
walking over to you
unable to hold itself back.

And you,
underneath
also leaving yourself.

There, in the center of the room
embracing in the empty space,

our love could not wait a moment longer
and is already one.

But we are still standing apart from one other
feeling the colder temperature
now that our second bodies have left us
and are making wild love in the center of the room.

We walk a step closer
as if standing near a fire
feeling the heat as our second bodies erupt into flame

and take another step
and allow ourselves to burn
until we too are on fire
and reach to touch one another
and our second bodies show us where to go.

How Unexplainable Was Our Joy?

I have written you, talked on the phone with you, texted
you, emailed you, spoken into the air knowing you could
hear me wherever you were, and dreamed about you.

Our breathing together was something other than life.
It was a waking dream.

I would get in my car to go to work and do the other
routine things of the day, like laundry and paying bills,
but always, there was a hovering joy that would take me
around and dance.

When we were together, it didn't matter if we were
shopping for food or clothes. It was like being on
vacation in the most exotic island in the world. We would
walk down the main aisle at the clothing store and I
would look over to see your profile and watch how you
walked. You would turn and smile.

That was it. I was in heaven. A feeling of joy would rub
up against every corner of my insides. I never came down.

When we were at the cash register paying for what we
had bought, I'd watch and listen as you talked with the
cashier.

Whether it was a man or a woman...
you would open a little part of them up...
and share a moment of sweetness together.

And I would think... you are so funny, self-deprecating,
and kind... to everyone,

and then you would turn, and smile at me, and I would
remember we were together and loved one another,
and I would have to stop myself from crying.

When we walked out the front door of the clothing store,
I held the door for you and you held the door for me,
and we walked a hundred feet to the car,
and I felt like the luckiest man in the world.

When we got in the car and closed the door, it was quiet.
I looked over at you and you smiled at me and then we
kissed each other and said, "I love you," and forgot that
we were in the car and were just intoxicated with love.
You said we should probably turn the car on so we could
go home and we laughed and drove home.

This is what I mean.
Every moment, a waking dream.
How unexplainable was our joy?

The Bend in the Grass

The curve in the field of the tall grass and you,
arching back like the mountain under my skin,
soft like the full weight of earth and scent.

Standing in our celestial glow,
our union
sweeps through the icy brightness
of rivers and trees.

We embrace in the clouds,
falling softly as snow,
and walk hand in hand, silent.

Oh, my gentle tall grass bending in the field!
Arching back like the mountain under my skin.

What is holding us so close?
Our burning turns white,
and trees shake in the wind.

Shhh... right here.

Yes?
My hands are warm.
Like falling leaves you whisper.
Now?
Yes.

How You Came into the World

"How did they do it?"
I asked the old tree, but she just smiled.

I leaned into her hard bark and said,
"I know you're in there,"
and heard a nearby stream laugh in the sun.

"How did they do it?" I asked again. "I have to know!"
Finally the old grandmother tree leaned in and whispered,
"Shhh..." and held me in her branches.

Flower petals floated from the sky
and a gentle shape began to unfold in the wind.

"Stop, stop," I said to grandmother tree.
"You cannot make one as beautiful as her!"
But it was too late. You were already here.

The Flower of Your Garden

Entering through the fire of your door,
into the gentle flower of your garden,
your soft body wraps around mine
like a warm bath of ecstasy.

The heat of your loins
sparks a fire through the rivers of my blood
and our warm lips press softly in yearning surrender.

You are the one I love, my darling!
Your voice, like the ocean washing over my skin.
Your arms, like the sun embracing earth.

We are the forest flooding the world,
our soft screams of surrender
open the gates
like water washing over the stones in the river.

She's Here

When you were born,
the angels spoke...

I was just a kid, playing on the front lawn.

"She's here..." they whispered.

"What?" I wondered.

But now I know.

You pour the coffee and turn, smiling.
I'm sitting on the couch.

"You are here," I say.

"Of course I'm here," you answer.
"Where else would I be?"

And then, I look at you and know...
I have loved you forever.

Two Souls

You found me on a small painted tile in the
sand and brought me into the world.

I found you in a golden dragonfly
and set it free.

Mother Goddess

You walk without affectation.
Your hair is simply brushed.
Your shoes are flats, or boots if it's cold.

You speak with the wisdom of simplicity,
and listen to every soul.
You kneel to hold the hands of children,
and reach up to speak with God.

You plant flowers in spring,
make meals and clean the floors,
wash and dry and fold the clothes,
and part the curtains for morning light.

You sit at the table,
preparing your family for life,
in ways that could never be counted,
and replenish the candles of their heart,
with the burning fire of yours.

Light is shining through your skin
and sun behind your eyes,
and for a moment, I forget you are a mother,
and see only the goddess inside.

On the Wind

My wings sail down as autumn leaves,
and float along the river of your valley.
We wake together,
as silent lightning upon the garden,
and clear running reflections of sun,
in wild water sparkling.

Leaf

Unfolding her nakedness
wholly exposed and vulnerable,
she reaches for the open heart of the sky
and gives of her rich green,
until silently one cold morning,
she returns like a delicate sunset,
home.

Vista

When the vista is too beautiful to take in,
it is like looking at you.

I Am Shifting

I am shifting.
Where I am, where my spirit lies.
No longer in the deep unspoken mystery.

No longer in the sacred text of ancients,
no longer in the still peace of fire's last breath. I am moving.

Into words and things and chatter streams flooding
into tires and gas pumps clicking off
pulling receipts out with a tearing sound healthy and loud.

There is an ocean I have hidden from
rotating on a spit over the world,
alive with so much life that it is dripping into the universe.

Now I will cook with the juicy meat, and sizzle on earth.

"Yes yes," I will say and hand a man a dollar,
and walk hard concrete with the world.

A cave shelters from the storm,
but when the storm is over, it is time to come out.

I never came out, through the seasons of life,
and thought perhaps darkness was my mother.

I don't know who you are,
but somehow you are inside me like a fish hook,
reeling me out into the light,
and perhaps I will die,

but reeling through this moment towards you,
is like the knowing I have never known,
made real, a thousand times over,
until there is no room for anything but joy.

I Loves a Woman

I loves a woman.
She make my life right.
I dream o' her all the time.

She take care o' her kids good.
She drives 'em everywhere they needs.
She feeds 'em,
makes sure they's doing what they should.

She tall like a goddess.
She soft like a goddess.
When she walks, it take my breath away.

Jus' to see her,
make me love 'er more,
and sometimes she come close,
and let me know,
this time's fer us,
and tears spill right out,

'cause I never had
the love pour in,
like a pitcher full o' water
on a hot day, till I's right full,

an' can't stop smiling,
'cause she's still there,
glowing like the sun.

The Joy of My Morning

You know,
I still wake up every morning with love songs in my heart.

Is that why I met you?
So that every morning I could wake up remembering the
beauty of our love? Or is it so that I could write day after day
what it feels like to be pulled towards joy?

There are so many futures that await.
It's like making magic potions
and deciding which one to pick.
I look at all the glass flasks, each one filled with a dream.

This one is blue
and I will become the sky and the birds.
This one is green
and I will become the forest and the animals.
This one is red
and I will become a warrior and spill the blood of my enemies.
This one is yellow
and I will become the flowers and bring beauty into the world.
This one is purple
and I will become a king and serve the needs of my people.
This one is orange
and I will become the sun and warm the Earth.

And this one is clear with no color at all.
If I drink this, I am free.

And that is the flask I choose. I drink.
I pour one drop around every inch of my house.
And one flower grows where every drop falls.

My insides have become like spring and I walk
full of hope, spilling over with pollen.

I am walking down the road to the golden treasure.
It is a beautiful path. It winds around the mountains and
down into the valleys.

There are wide rivers to cross,
and sometimes the food is scarce,
but most of the time it is a good path,

filled with passers-by
and we hold up our hands to wave,
and wish each other well,
because we know how much we dream.

And sometimes we stop and make a fire together.
roasting marshmallows,
because we still remember
when we were children and held sticks,

and were allowed for the first time
to cook our food in the fire,
and not just any food but a sweet dessert,
until it was just about to burn because it got so hot.

But we learned to pull it away before it turned black,
and even then, it tasted good, because the insides were soft
and creamy and warm like the soft sea and earth
smoothing our heart.

That is how it feels being near the heat of you.
Like smoothing out my insides until there are no more
ragged bumps and edges, or worry, or want.
When I am near the heat of you,
there is only the soft warmth of knowing, I am home.

And in the morning I kiss you until you laugh and say,
"Stop!" because I am kissing you all over,
and we make eggs and toast and look at the river.

We meet our friends and they smile,
wondering how it happened...
One of them pulls me aside and says,

"You know,
I thought in my heart there was really no way,
but I was so wrong, and I just wanted to tell you,
you have shown me the power of love."

And I say,

"Every day I am walking as an angel,
slightly above the ground,
and every breath is like the scent of a flower,
and every beat of my heart
is like ringing the bell
that began the world."

Warm Earth

Morning comes with soft feet.
She brings her rain.
She brings her sun.
Waiting for you to open.

Mirror

She tries on the universe.
It fits so well.
She looks in the mirror and smiles at herself
covered in stars and light
and turns to me and says, "I love it!"

Waking

The stars of night,
the clear songs of birds,
snow's gentle fall to earth.

My skin trembles near the heat of you
and the warm river underneath.

I yearn to taste the sweet fruit
and ache to pound the plains like drums.

A Note

I know you are coming so what can I give you?
Just these words, Darling.

I love you.

The world is filled with utter joy
and every thought feels like the warm sea.

When the wind blows,
your name brushes through,
and when the river swims,
I hear your heart singing.

At night, the stars ask if they can visit.
I tell them "Yes of course, come visit with us together."
They tell me how lucky I am.

Everything is talking to me.
The grass and the trees,
the birds fluttering by the window,
and even the fireflies at night.

And my heart…
my heart beats the very sound
of your breath as if you are inside me.

What shall I do with this chorus of life singing?

Whisper

Holding the paintbrush of air and trees,
she paints her essence around my skin
whispering the secrets of grass and sky.

Across the lakes and rivers,
across the roads and cities,

I dream
of rushing waters
and wildflowers blowing

as she gathers us
into the basket of branches
and runs into the wind.

When the bones are made,

they are made a certain way.
And usually, they stay that way.

And you walk and talk for a long time.
But sometimes someone comes into your life
and even your bones are changed
and you can never walk the same way again.

While driving down the highway I saw the clouds

and thought of you. How you open your wings
and lift away from earth like a great heron.

It is such a beautiful sight
when you lift into the sky,

like the tall grass blowing in the fields
or the way the waves begin to curl.

And when I see you flying away,
the sea of my heart spills out
because then I know you are a real angel,

not the imaginary one in children's story books,
but the one that actually came
and made a fire in my life.

Even the Birds Fly Close

The river of your heart swims through the light of this day,
and the breath of your flower opens my morning eyes.

You take my face in your hands and pull me to you.
I am no longer separate from the pulse of your life.

The running deer do not know
you are warming them with the spring of your joy,

and the squirrels do not know
you are holding them as they jump
from branch to branch,

but I do,
and laugh with every tree
and even the birds fly close.

No One Will Understand

No one will understand unless I tell them.

"It is like this," I say.

Imagine you were lying in the underworld,
forgotten,

even to yourself.

And imagine that in the darkness
a ray of sun appeared.

And imagine that the ray of sun
materialized in front of you and took your hand.

And imagine that the ray of sun was an angel
and spoke your name and held you gently
until your strength returned and you could stand again,

and feel your own heart beating
and know what really happened;

That life had given you every dream
but that you had become lost.

And what if this angel then fed you,
and began the arduous task
of carrying you up from the black center of your prison
into a light that you had never known,

and brought you to a lake
shining with reflections of sun so brightly
that it was like a thousand suns sparkling on the water,

and the geese flew by calling you to come
and the trees beckoned
and you knew this was the brightest day of your life,

and what if just when you thought you could not burn
more brightly, the angel came close and held you,

and breathed her breath into you
until every cell inside sparked with life
and you felt like you were the rush of birth itself,

and for the first time in your life
knew what it was to be alive.

What Light Is

When I look up in the night sky,
it is clear that the stars and I are brothers
and I feel the warmth of their light in my heart.

In the morning, the sun streaks through the leaves
and says, "I am here."

When the sun comes like this,
softly warm and comforting,
I understand what the birds are saying
and even the silence of the rocks on the hillside.

And because the sun has come,
there is something else I understand.

Now, when I look at you
I see the deeper sun,
the sun that is inside the fire of all life,
burning in your eyes.

Sense

I touch
your skin with gentle hands,
like the sea brushing the soft shore.

I hear
your breath rush past my ears
like the warm wind of spring
breaking through winter's frozen stillness.

I smell
your scent as sweat glistens
like mountain runoff filling lakes and rivers.

I see
the sun rising in your eyes,
opening like morning.

I taste
the sweetness of our bond,
like fruit in the warmth of the valley.

Sails in the Wind

"Heading out," I said,
and felt you exploding like the creation of the world.

"Meet me!" you exclaimed.

"Yes, yes!" … I cannot get there fast enough.

And waiting, waiting in the field under the stars,
as if you were the present
I have waited my whole life to open.

Suddenly, you are by my side,
our union, sacred.

We sing like children,
discovering their hands can move,
and even shape the world.

And race out,
like horses from the gate,
across towns and villages.

Flying…flying now we are,
steadying our wings, and landing in the field…

Joining all life…

sitting together in a circle around the burning fire.

I remember!

You were always by my side.

We chant into the deep night
rekindling our ancient promise.

And laughter... laughter runs up and down the hills,
and dreams parade on the tips of the fire,
like hope knowing it will live forever,

embracing every soul until the leaves fall,
and we two still on the tree of breath and water,
swimming home with the blue edge of night
along our slippery sides.

The soft dream, the end of edges and borders,
falling into the lakes of each other,
until we are the water and the moon above.

Circling Love

Why does your heart circle like a full moon?
Why does your heart dance in my soul?

And why, when I have gotten used
to the soft feeling of honey in my blood,
has your love come into my breath?

Dancing and swimming
like a sweet and beautiful fish,
waving its body back and forth, back and forth...

softly circling in and out
like a paddle wheel,
plunging into the cool water
and rising up to the sun.

Your love circles through my body,
it knows the song of my heart
and they sing together.

The warm sweetness of it runs up to my fingers
and down to my feet,
and up through my chest,
and down to my legs.

Like a glowing river
it breathes me into life
as if I were the beginning of day, rising to the sun
like a flower that never stops opening.

The Language of Water and Thirst

We spoke the language of water and thirst
as I brushed my face against yours,
and breathing softly by your ear,
unfolded the silence.

I opened your palm and
your mouth full of scent and honey
and you opened your vulnerable softness
and left me gasping quietly in tears.

Like waves of nature, your breasts
poured into the soft places of my bones
and my skin surrendered near the radiant heat
of your giving thighs.
I dreamed as I ran my fingers through your hair
like walking through the promise of spring.

I took your small feet in my hands and pressed
the strength of my heart into your gentle soles,
and all the hidden gates opened. The sun glowed
from within your body, my hands, our breathing.

Touching the delicate landscape of your back, I
kneaded and released the tight parts of living that
wanted to be free, and listened to the soft gasps,
like waves of yearning, finding their home over
and over, and you turned and could not wait any
longer, could not withstand the yearning waves
touching home, and fell into the place where
memory is forgotten and warm rain falls from sun.

Flower in the Field

Between this day and death there is only you
like a flower in the field
with open arms.

At moments like this I more than love you.
I weep for the gift of you in my life.

Overcome with your eyes and words,
overcome with the way you have held me in your heart
and the way you have taken me into your arms.

Oh sweet woman of earth
you are a glowing ember of the goddess.

To feel your touch is to be reborn with every breath.

I dance and cry and sing
and hold you wrapped like a vine loving its tree
around your vulnerable softness
and the whisper of your surrender spreads through me
like the first rain of spring

and we open together,
like a thousand flowers,
spilling into the field.

Her Light

We swim through the waves of day,
and fall into the soft blanket of night.

She takes me into her space
and the stars pulse so comfortably.
They know the sway of her hips
and breathe with the heat of her rhythm.

She sings with the wind and dances with the sea.

There is nothing I can do, to stand tall enough by her side,
by the queen, the goddess, the maker of life,
even in the darkest valley,
she dances in her light.

I dance with her and she asks how to return home.
I am so thankful I remember the way
and show her how to step into the clouds.

Like a deer she leaps into the sky,
and her colors glow like every flower blooming.

I don't know if I am worthy to be with her
and kneel as she opens her wings,
and looks to Heaven's godly sun.

I have been graced to protect her, to bring her home
and perhaps I will be told to return,
but she touches my bowed head and lifts my face to hers,
and there is a river in her eyes.

On earth, she holds me, in our bed, in our heat.
We say, "Oh God," and pour into one another.

I look at her the next day striding to the car and bending
over to put a box in the back seat. I grab her from behind
and she laughs and says, "Stop," and I feel the heat of her
softness and she turns to me and says, "Don't stop,"
and I kiss her hard and she says, "How much time do we
have?" and I say, "Not enough," and she smiles and says,
"I'll be back," and I say, "You better come back!" and she
says, "You're killing me, you know that?"

And I can't let her go, but she wiggles her softness and
drives off. I'm standing there alone, and look up at the sun,
and know that she is in there too, and say to the sun,

"Thanks a lot,
how am I supposed to be able to function now?"

And I feel the heat of the sun,
so much like her walk, her touch,
and know she is still with me, and I smile,
and must finally give up.

That's it, I just give up trying to understand why the world
is spinning, and I am dizzy and I try my best to walk into
the next step of my day without her, and I do,
and all day repeat under my breath,

"Oh my God..."

I drive to work and say "Hi" to my co-workers
and everyone around me smiles,
and I say "What?"
and they say, "You crazy boy!"

But I'm a man, and they know I'm hopelessly in love,
as if I was sixteen, but even they are starting to glow a
little as the sway of her hips shakes through me.

And although they can't see my insides glowing,
they're smiling, as if the gift of her womanhood
is glowing inside them too.

I'm almost unable to pay attention to anything,
but somehow manage to get through the day,
finish my work, and say good-bye.

I return home and moments later,
a car comes up the gravel drive.
I look through the window,
and drink in the joy of seeing her.

And as she walks away from the car I see her movement,
her goddess life-giving hips sway with her walk
and I cannot move fast enough to be with her.

*W*ashing through my core

the last stream passes through.
I have become an empty vessel,
ready to leave this old tree.

But from somewhere unknown,
the heat of you comes
like wind
touching every leaf.

$\mathcal{A}$ poet cannot provide food, clothing, or shelter.

You will die suffering in rags while the poet writes.

A carpenter will build a house,
A doctor will stitch a wound,
A farmer will grow food.

But a poet will love you forever.

The Light in Her Hand

We are holding hands through the jail of her life.
"Go... leave me," She says.
But I will not leave my angel.

I am standing on the soft grass by the edge of the lake.
Sparkles are dancing like little flecks of gold on the water.
She is dancing on the water.

The wind blows towards me,
and the little flecks of gold come closer.
The geese are honking.
They fly over my head with a whoop whoop sound
and splash into the cool water.

The angel dances towards me.
I'm not supposed to hug and kiss the angel, but I do.
Heart of my heart she is - I touch her face and she cries.
The lake sparkles in the arms of the sun.

The geese flap and honk on the water.

I step back to look at her.
Her wings, her heart, her eyes opening into heaven.

And then she is gone.

Where Are You?

Where are you, my darling?
I am searching for you.

In my dreams,
while driving to work
or writing on my bed
or on my chair by the little table
in the center of the room
or eating breakfast
on the roof of the old house
or standing on the dock.

Where are you?
I hear your voice
and remember its gentle sound
and think of your heart
and how when I kiss you,
I dissolve.

Because when I am with you
time stops
and I can hear my heart
talking to me
telling me
I am home.

Clear Light

We will never know
why the current was so fierce,
the wind so strong,
and the sun so bright

but it was
and we were the lucky ones
who felt all of it

and rejoiced
in our breath,
in waking every day,
to a miracle

that could only be given to us
and we shall have that forever.

Watering the Plants

When I do little things around the house now,
I remember how you would have done it,

and of course, thinking of you makes me cry,
because you are no longer here, and sometimes I just...

Oh, Darling... Is this what it's like?

We drank coffee together, got dressed, went to work,
made dinner, read to one another, and when we played
scrabble, you always beat me.

The only way I could win was if you allowed it,
or helped me, and you always did.

But I still feel you, putting your hand over my hand
as I pour the water in the coffee maker.

I feel you like a warm coat
and hear the whisper of your voice
in every corner of the room.

Underneath

Innocently unfolding
nurtured by the water
wind and sun

we grew
as young plants
and then
great trees

and one day
changed
and were free to move

and to our surprise
found
we had wings
and flew so high
we touched the stars

and there
in the clear light

remembered who we were
and came back
to say goodbye.

What You Don't Know...

...Is that the little boy...
painted on the small tile you found in the sand
still touches my heart

inspiring dreams to bloom
from the center of nowhere,
and is still propped up
on the mantle above the old fireplace.

I make my bed and leave everything just as you left it
so if you should decide to put your key in the door...

...the key that I gave you, saying
"Come into my life,"
that the room will still be holding its arms open to you,
welcoming you home.

And we will once again unfold as two prayers,
sailing through the sky.

Every Morning

Little bird, why do you come,
every morning when I wake,
singing songs like little drops of sunlight?

I am drinking in every sweet note
as I watch you on my window ledge.

Sometimes you fly around the room.
Can you not become human
and tell me who you are?

Oh little bird, I remember!
You did become human once!

You were so much bigger then.
Your colors were flaming orange and red
and you would look at me for a long time,

and then
take a step closer
like a flamingo or a great heron
and your long legs suddenly looked like a woman's.
I followed them up past your feathers
and looked at your face.

Though you came as a bird
who kept her freedom,
you now had hair like golden fields
and eyes like the gentle sea.

I kissed you
and your feathers fell away
decorating the floor like shells on the sand
and the waves from the beach came right into the room.

They came through,
again and again,
through you,
through me.

What was that?
Which had no word or time,
and dissolved every cell
until we became the sea and the wind.

Oh great bird who comes,
changing and walking,
who puts on the body of a woman
for a little while

who sheds her wings
and holds me in the cover of her arms
and lets me see her face,
radiant like the sun.

I cannot stay in my body feeling this bliss
and then, you are a little bird again,
sitting on my window ledge, and flit away.

The Way You Loved Me Then

See me like you saw me then,
when I was an angel.

Wrestle me to the ground laughing.
Don't let me up until you've had your way.

Remember when I was made from lightning and sun?
How fiercely you wielded your sword then.

And how I died in bliss,
under the weight of your warm softness,
and tumbled out of my skin,

to became sun and leaves,
on the river of your unbridled passion,

and could no longer open my eyes,
or remember my name.

Sun Cloud

You gathered the stones from the river
and placed them

in a circle... under the trees.

The wind came
and touched the ground.

The animals came
and stood around the edge
of the circle
and said,
this is your space.

When the fields were resting
from the work of our hands
and the work of the sun,

we came...
I first, and then...

I heard your footsteps,
and cawed like a crow.
You stepped into the circle of stones

and wrapped the world around me
like a blanket from the sky
and I touched the places
that made us dream.

I wash the stones in the river
and hear your wings beat against the sky

and look up
as you turn into the sun.

The Veil

Before you drew the veil between us,
I was a passionate fire
burning in the heart the forest

and you could not understand
the warm waves spreading
through every pore of your skin.

- Forget what I have become -
- my plain existence -

and remember
when my wings were soft

and the wind wrapped around us
and I covered you
with the heat of my life.

A Patient Cloud

You breathed the air of plains and sky,
and I, of sand and shore.

You painted pictures of open doors.
I sang of what was lost.

We swam like fish across the ocean,
and returned to our native homes.

And settled with spouses and children's songs,
weekends, dishes and sweeping the floor,

and years later, found one another.
You touched my arm and said,

"I think you need a comma here,"
and all the flowers opened.

We painted our dreams on one another,
and dissolved in the morning sun.

Afterglow

When the door opens
you may expect to see a floor and a ceiling.
Are you satisfied? Is that enough?

Please, come near.
I am whispering in your ear.

There was love here once.
The walls have been painted and the trim is white.

But can you see into the center of the room?
It is still burning there, brighter than the sun.

To Look at a Room

There were parts of us all over the room.
On the desk, the bed, the floor.
We were like cans of paint mixed together.

We danced in the center like two suns.

What we shared cannot be named.
More than love, more than laughter,
more than words, or touching.

It was the rushing river that came through the windows,
and we screamed with joy as it ran through.

Soft Mourning

It would be easier to never wake,
when it is so hard to live,
waiting like a trapped animal in your skin.

Like a fish losing the rainbow of its life
or a bird fluttering on the grass with a broken wing.

Her light appears in dream
but waking finds only the clothes she left behind.

The things she touched
still shine with the spark of life

but all the gentle flowers inside your heart are dying
and you weep and cannot stop,

because you lost
the most beautiful moment of your life.

Soft Cloth and Canvas

I am emptying your studio
of all your possessions,
all that you touched,
blessed, and painted.

Guessing

how to place the shapes of your life
in the van,
so nothing will be damaged.

I carry them out
like sacred gifts.

You will be here soon,
to survey the last of your things
and take them home.

In between this moment of helping you move,
and the rest of our lives, the world is opening,
returning to the sea.

I will stand by the edge of the water
and call your name forever.

Wind and Water

The river floods its banks searching for us
and the wind peels back the leaves of the trees
looking to see where the glow of our flame has gone.

We run and laugh and hide
and rest in the soft warmth of our arms.
But in the stillness of our dreams, we are awakened.
The wind and the water are talking outside our hiding place.
They have found us...

You, who love one another with the glow of the sun

    ...listen...

In the morning it is still.
My love goes out and talks to the water.
I go out to join her but she is gone.

In My Bones

I am sailing
across the sky
in the current
of your soft breath,

obedient
to your wish...

I will leave...

and find someone else
under the sun.

I will trick myself into believing
I cannot live without them,

but in my bones,
my honest bones,
not the ones you say I should have,

but the ones I really have,
in those bones,
your name is written
forever.

The Winds of Fall

The last traces of fall push past the windows moaning.
I know the cry of that hollow sound.

I cup my hands around our dream, like a little flame,
but the wind blows everything away
and I am left behind, after the harvest, kneeling in the field.

"Those crops will never come back," the cold earth says.

"I know," I answer.

"Go home," the earth says. "Go home."

I lie in bed,
and cry with the haunting wind.

Endings

Hold your breath.
Say good-bye.

Why am I so afraid of endings?

The carnival ride is over,
college is over,
your career is over,
your marriage is over,
your partner has passed away.

Your parents are hanging on the wall.
I am ending. The universe is ending.

Something has pulled away.

Like the end of summer.
like an empty room, an empty bed.

Like packing up from vacation,
leaving something beautiful behind,
a tree, a flower, your beloved,
your heart.

$\mathcal{T}$he sun rests upon the world

the river is running,
nothing is still,
except my heart,
waiting to understand.

Come Back to Me

Come back to me.
Throw off your chains
and rip down the sails that are blowing you away.
Jump off the side of the boat if you have to and swim.

Run out the front door and don't look back.
Get in your car and floor it.
Walk away from your desk and don't wait for the elevator.
Run down the stairs and out the door.

Drop the coffee cup in your hand.
Call me now and tell me you are coming back.
Weep into the phone
and tell me your heart has exploded like a tidal wave.
Text me that you are on your way
and cannot get here fast enough.

I will drop the wrench in my hand.
I will drop the calculations in my head.
I will say, *excuse me* to the person I am with
and run to my car.

I will race like a madman to come to you.
I will barely be able to keep my heart in my chest
and all my old dreams will be waking up
like a thousand flowers bursting through the ground.

Oh, how I will kiss you,
throw you on the bed and ravish you
and how you will grab and grasp me
trying to pull me into you.

And the room will be catching on fire with our heat
and our spirits will leave our bodies and crash back
into them again and again
and we will pass through earth screaming in ecstasy

and become a ball of sun
until every seed of life explodes
and lambs are born, and lions...
and whales plunge into the ocean
and the whole world cries with utter joy.

Harvest

The hay bales have been put up in the barn.
It is time for the horses to rest.
The stillness of the day spreads its silent peace
across the empty fields.

The aching bones,
the torn work clothes,
and the leaning wagons will be mended.

A chill arrives in the morning air
and fall begins its long slow breath
of goodbye.

Clear

I have put away all the navigational charts
and reference books
and even the spiritual texts.
I have put away the practices and the striving
to be a saint or God.

I have let everything go.

There...
all the possibilities
and choosing none of them.

I will only follow
the next bend of straw in the field
or ripple on the water.

The Geese on the Hill

Your spirit jumps and rings with joy.
Oh, how you love the geese!
Their soft footsteps make you laugh.
"They're tiptoeing with a secret!" you say.

But where are you, my love?
Are you in the grass?
Are you in the leaves?
Are you hidden in the wind?

Oh Dear! They're walking -
like the sweetest little army you ever saw,
one behind the other...

and their webbed feet make no sound,
and they do not honk,
or twitch nervously from side to side.

But I hear the wind through the leaves,
... your wind, the reminder of your heart.

And Sweetheart...!
There they are now,
at the end of the dock
comfortably gauging their stance,
taking perfect little hops into the water,

one, after another, after another,
wiggling their short little tails
and swimming off,
following nature's voice
until I can see them no more.

They are gone.
The mothers, the goslings,
the silent walk down the grassy hill.
I know they are on the lake somewhere past the trees.
I know they are there.

But I cannot wish them back
to sit next to me on the grass
where we shared a perfect moment in the sun,
where we could breathe together, feel the heat together,
and hear the low rustle of wind touching the trees.

What was between the silent march of their little feet
towards the water and my memory of you?

They are on the lake somewhere,
like you, heart of my heart.
I can no longer see them.
They are on the water swimming perfectly away.

$\mathcal{L}$ike leaves of fall
I surrender.

Our words whispered
across the giving earth

find their home
in silent mornings.

Still

You are in me.

Like my own heart beating.

Every moment.
Every breath.

While I sleep, live and die.

You are in me.

I cannot
stop thinking of you.

Like my own heart beating.

You are in me forever.

Your Voice

I hear you in the breath of my chest
and see you in the glow of the leaves.
Your paintings surround me with your open heart.

But you are no longer here.

You are getting the milk out of the refrigerator for your son
and reaching into the cabinet for the cereal box.
Your daughter is coming down the stairs,
and laughs because your son said

"I dreamed I was a seagull and showed everyone how to fly."

We live so near to one another.
I could drive over, or you could come to me,
but that cannot happen now.

You are still wearing the golden dragonfly around your neck,
and I am still holding the magical tile you found in the sand.

I'm looking at the lake through the sunlit leaves. It is spring.
You have returned home, and your children are laughing again.

I see the books on my table, the ones you bought for me
and remember when we read to one another.

By now, you've driven your daughter to work at the coffee shop.
You're talking and laughing with a few early morning customers.

"See ya later," you say to your daughter,
 and she smiles and says, "Bye, Mom."

You bring your son to the baseball game. He gets a hit.

This is what we do, our lives. The sun warms your skin.
You are reading and turn the page.

I hear birds chirping in the whispering trees.
Spring is blooming everywhere.

Your artwork and paintings glow in the soft morning.
The sunlight touches the books you bought for me
and in the stillness I hear your voice.

 "Read the books I gave you."

I do. Page after page your heart pours out.
I love you.
Everything I ever dreamed of came true.

Jeff Edrich is the author of three
collections of poems and stories:

Dream of Broken Feathers,
When the Sun Touched the River,
and *Iron in the Country*.

Born in Brooklyn and raised
in the suburban town of Matawan,
New Jersey, his lifelong contemplations
have helped him understand that life
is no longer a question to ponder,
but a gentle gift to be thankful for.

78912048R00069

Made in the USA
Lexington, KY
15 January 2018